Ledra's Book

Poems, Songs, Jingles, Genealogy, and Picture Book

Ledra A. White Lynch

by Luanna Lynch Leisure

Illustrated by Sharon Moran

Ledra's Book

ISBN: 978-0-578-16998-9

Published by Luanna K. Leisure, Campbell, California 95008.

Printed in the United States of America.

Illustrator: Sharon Thompson Moran, Visalia, California 93292. All illustrations © 2020.

Cover photo and title page photo taken on May 19, 1925, Ledra and Ethmer's Wedding Day, Fair Play, Missouri.

I have worked diligently to confirm material not composed by my mother is public domain and/or Creative Commons work.

To order additional books go to:
http://www.LuLu.com or Amazon.com

Email: LuannaLeisureBooks@aol.com
www.LuannaLeisureBooks.com

Little White Feather Publishing

Table of Contents

Table of Contents

Chapter

Dedicated to Our Mother,
Ledra Anita White Lynch

1909-2000

Compiled and Published by
Luanna Lynch Leisure
For My Brothers and Sisters

*James Lynch (1933-2020), Luanna Lynch Leisure, William "Bill" Lynch (1931-2011),
Barbara Lynch Gannaway (1926-2005), Sharyl Lynch Justice,
Belva Lynch Findley (1928-2016). c. January 2000.*

Special Appreciation and Gratitude

To my talented cousin, Sharon Thompson Moran, who painted and donated the fun artwork for her Aunt Ledra's book. Sharon's mother, Marilyn White Thompson was Ledra's youngest sister. Sharon, your art makes *Ledra's Book* complete.

I love you and appreciate you, Cousin!

Thank you!

To my sister, Sharyl Lynch Justice, for her help in remembering dates, stories, and family circumstances. What a joy it is to talk, laugh, and sometimes cry about our childhood days and growing into adults. I love and cherish the hours we spend on the phone together researching our family roots. Who would have guessed we both would grow up to be genealogists?

I love and appreciate you, Sister!

Thank You!

Cousins
Easter Sunday, 1960

Luanna Lynch,
Sharon Thompson,
Sharyl Lynch, and
Pam Thompson

Below
Jerrie Dixon Lynch,
Genealogist and
Author
1933-2019

I would very much be amiss if I didn't express my immense appreciation and gratitude to my sister-in-law, Geraldene "Jerrie" Golden Dixon Lynch, wife of James Lynch. She is the one who sparked the excitement in me to research our family roots, which we did together for hours at a time. Those hours we spent together are cherished times and wonderful memories.

I love, miss, and appreciate you, Sister!

Thank You!

Foreword

When I first compiled a book of my mother's poetry, songs, and jingles, all of my siblings were living. Now, my sister Sharyl and I are the only ones left. I had created the book for them, mainly to keep Mom's poetry, songs, and jingles that she loved in print so our family could remember what a fun, creative person she was. Another reason was to honor her for her achievement when she was only seven years old when she took second place in a grade-school contest (she didn't want to win first place). I wonder if, at the time, her family acknowledged her accomplishment.

Her teacher had her memorize a portion of a book, *Mary Cary* by Kate Langley Bosher, published in 1910. As a note of interest, Kate Langley Bosher was a suffragist and founding member and officer of the Equal Suffrage League of Virginia.

From the time I have memories of Mom reciting her poetry, she would recite this funny, adorable story. She would even act it out as if she were Mary Cary. In 1993, before Mom became too forgetful, (even though her poetry she seemed to always remember) I sat down with her and, as she recited, I wrote. I then compiled a folder with her writings and added photos and clip art, and I mailed a copy to each of my siblings along with the book *Mary Cary*. To find books for everyone, I had to go online to bookstores all across the U.S.

At first, I didn't know *Mary Cary* was a book. When I went to a library and requested the recital story of *Mary Cary*, I was informed it was an actual book. This surprised me. Mom never said it was from a book. Maybe she didn't know. After all, she was only seven.

I've decided to name this book, *Ledra's Book.* She once told me, "None of you named your babies after me." I didn't want to hurt her by saying she had a very different name, one I didn't want my daughter to have. "I'm sorry, Mom." So, now I wish I could tell her about my new book. To honor my mother, the title is *Ledra's Book.* I didn't name my daughter after her, but any author knows that by the time you finish a book it is your baby. I think she would be pleased.

In the pages of *Ledra's Book* are original poetry and songs written by my mother. Also included are jingles and songs she learned as a child that I could, at any moment of the day, hear her belt out with joy and gusto. Mom always had a poem or song in her heart, even when her heart was sad.

I've added photographs of Ledra's life along with my memoirs and thoughts. Also included are my sister Sharyl's memories of Mom and memories from her grandchildren.

I have worked diligently to confirm material not composed by my mother is public domain and/or Creative Commons work.

Albert and Vinnie Harsh White

Ledra's Family c. 1916, Mt. Ayr, Iowa

Top left to right: Ina and Earl

Middle: Vinnie, Clarice, and Albert

Elvis on his mother's lap,

Harry Oliver "Bob," and Ledra.

Note: Albert and Vinnie had thirteen children. Eleven lived to be adults. Two did not have children. Nine of their children blessed them with 33 grandchildren.

I

Mary Cary

Mom, "Ledra," was seven years old when her teacher gave her an assignment to memorize a portion of *Mary Cary* for a county recital contest. Her teacher came and told her they were deciding between her and a younger boy. They finally came to her and said she won second place. Mom was so happy because she didn't want to go on to Des Moines for the state contest. She wanted to go home to her mama and daddy.

Ledra didn't win that contest, but she won the hearts of many, including me, throughout her life by reciting *Mary Carey* over and over again. She would perform for the senior citizen's center, at home for friends and company, and, many times, just because she loved to recite.

Luanna

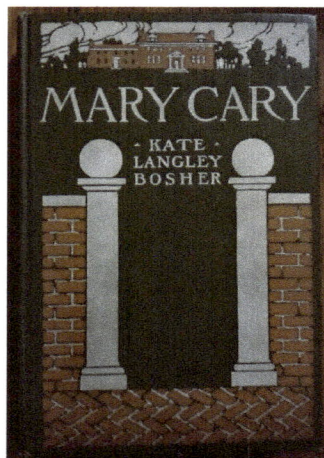

Mary Cary

Excerpts from the book
Published February 1910
by Kate Langley Bosher

My name is Mary Cary. I live in the Yorkburg Female Orphan Asylum. You may think nothing happens in an Orphan Asylum. It does. The orphans are sure enough children, and real much like the kind that have mothers and fathers.

Today I was kept in. Yesterday, too. The reason I was kept in was this. Miss Bray says it was for impertinence.

It was this way. In the summer we have much more time than in the winter, and the children kept coming to me asking me to make up something, and all of a sudden a play came in my mind. I just love acting. The play was to be the marriage of Dr. Rudd and Miss Bray.

You see, Miss Bray is dead in love with Dr. Rudd. And whenever he comes to see any of the children who are sick she is so solicitous and sweet and smiley that we call her, Ipecac Mollie. Other days, plain Mollie Cottontail. It seemed to me if we could just think him into marrying her, it would be the best work we'd ever done. And not liking Dr. Rudd, we didn't mind thinking her on him. Every day we'd meet for an hour and think together, and each one promised to think single, and in between times we got ready.

She is fifty-three years old, and all frazzled out and done up with adjuncts. But Dr. Rudd, being a man with not even usual sense, and awful conceited, don't see what

Ledra A. White
Abt. 7 yrs. old.

3

Mary Cary

we see, and swallows easy. Men are funny – funny as some women.

I don't think he's ever thought of courting Miss Bray. But she's thought of it, and for once we truly tried to help her.

On the fourth of July I made a New-Year resolution. I resolved I would do those things I should not do, and leave undone the things I should. I would not disappoint Miss Bray. She looked for things in me to worry her. She should find them.

But the play was a corker; it certainly was. We chose Friday night because Miss Bray goes to choir practicing. The ceremony took place in the basement-room where we play in bad weather. It's a right nice place to march in, being long and narrow.

I was the preacher and Prudence Arch and Nita Polley, Emma Clark and Margaret Witherspoon were bridesmaids.

Lizzie Wyatt was the bride, and Katie Freeman, who is the tallest girl in the house, though only fourteen, was the groom.

Katie is so thin she would do as well for one thing in this life as another, so we made her Dr. Rudd.

We didn't have but two men. Miss Webb says they're really not necessary at weddings, except the groom and the minister. Nobody notices them, and, besides, we couldn't get the pants.

I was an Episcopal minister, so I wouldn't need any. Mrs. Blamire's raincoat was the gown, and I cut up an old petticoat into strips, and made bands to go down the front and around my neck. Loulie Prentiss painted some crosses and marks on them with gilt, so as to make me look like a Bishop. I did. A little cent one.

There wasn't any trouble about my costume, because I could soap my hair and make it lie flat, and put on the robe, and there I was. But how to get a pair of pants for Katie Freeman was a puzzle.

I went out in the yard where a man was painting a window-shutter that had blown off a back window. Right before my eyes was the woodhouse door wide open, and something said to: "walk in."

4

I walked in; and there in a corner on a woodpile was a real nice pair of pants and a collar. And when I saw those pants I knew Katie Freeman was fixed.

They belonged to the man who was painting the shutter. It was an awful hot day, and he had taken them off in the woodhouse and put on his overalls, and when he wasn't looking I slipped out with them, and went up to Miss Bray's room. She was down-stairs talking to Miss Jones, and I hid them under the mattress of her bed.

I knew when she found they were missing she'd turn to me to know where they were. No matter what went wrong, from the cat having kittens or the chimney smoking, she looked to me as the cause. And if there was to be any searching, No. 4 – I sleep in No. 4 when Miss Katherine is away - would be the first thing searched. So I put them under her bed.

He is young, and Bermuda Ray says he is in love with Callie Payne, who lives just down the street. He has to pass her house going home, and I guess that's the reason he wore his good clothes and took them off so carefully. But whether that was it or not, he was the rippenest, maddest man I ever saw in my life when he went to put on his pants and there were none to put.

I almost rolled off the porch up-stairs, where I was watching. I never did know before how much a man thinks of his pants. And he settled himself on the woodpile to wait until dark before he went home.

When the bride and groom and the bridesmaids came in, all the girls were standing in rows on either side of the walls, making an aisle in between, and they sang a wedding song I had invented from my heart.

It was to the Lohengrin tune, which is a little wobbly for words, but they got them in all right, keeping time with their hands. These are the words:

1

Here comes the Bride,

God save the Groom!

And please don't let any chil-i-il-dren come,

For they don't know

How children feel,

Nor do they know how with chil-dren to deal.

2

She's still an old maid,

Though she would not have been

Could she have mar-ri-ed any kind of man.

But she could not.

So to the Humane

She came, and caus-ed a good deal of pain.

3

But now she's here

To be married, and go

Away with her red-headed, red-bearded beau.

Have mercy, Lord,

And help him to bear

What we've been doing this many a year!

And such singing! We'd been practicing in the back part of the yard, and humming in bed, so as to get the words into the tune; but we hadn't let out until that night. That night we let go.

There's nothing like singing from your heart, and, though I was the minister and stood on a box which was shaky, I sang, too. I led.

And that bride! She was Miss Bray. A graven image of her couldn't have been more like her.

She was stuffed in the right places, and her hair was frizzed just like Miss Bray's frizzed in front, and slick and tight in the back; and her face was a purple pink, and powdered all over, with a piece of dough just above her mouth on the left side to correspond with Miss Bray's mole.

And she held herself so like her, shoulders back, and making that little nervous sniffle with her nose, like Miss Bray makes when she's excited.

The groom didn't look like Dr. Rudd. But she wore men's clothes, and that's the only way you'd know some men were men, and almost anything will do for a groom. Nobody noticed him.

We were getting on just grand, and I was marrying away, telling them what they must do and what they mustn't. And then I turned to the bride.

"Miss Bray," I said, "have you told this man you are marring that you are two-faced and underhand, and can't be trusted to tell the truth? Have you told him that nobody loves you, and that for years you have tried to pass for a lamb, when you are an old sheep? And does he know that though you're a good manager on little and are not lazy, that your temper's been ruined by economizing, and that at times, if you were dead, there'd be no place for you? Peter wouldn't pass you, and the devil wouldn't stand you. And does he know he's buying a pig in a bag, and that the best wedding present he could give you would be a set of new teeth? And will you promise to stop pink powder and clean your finger-nails, every day? And _____."

But I got no further, for something made me look up, and there, standing in the door, was the real Miss Bray.

All I said was – "Let us pray!"

Footnote: At the top of page 4, third paragraph, is a sentence that reads: "I resolved I would do those things I should not do, and leave undone the things I should."

This may not be true, but for the first time, at the age of 72, a lightbulb clicked on in my brain. I see a similarity to something Mom always said to me when I would protest about a spanking for which I was sure I was innocent.

When I yelled in protest as she was spanking me, she would say, "I would rather spank you for something you didn't do than to let you go undone for something you did do."

Certainly sounds similar, doesn't it?   *Luanna*

First Five Children of Albert and Vinnie White
Top left to right: Harry Oliver "Bob," Ina, and Earl
Front: Ledra and Clarice
c. 1915 Mount Ayr, Ringgold Co., Iowa

Girlfriends c. late 1922, Fair Play, Missouri
Ledra White, Della Berry, and Vaughn Taylor
How pretty! I can imagine them dancing the Charleston and having fun.
Mom loved the Charleston and would dance around the house when I was a
teenager. She once took a puff of Dad's cigarette and danced for my
girlfriends. My jaw dropped. I couldn't believe that was my mom.

Boyfriend
Girlfriend

c. 1924
Fair Play, Cedar County,
Missouri

Ledra White and
Ethmer Lynch

Albert and Vinnie White
Move from Iowa to Missouri c. 1922

As told to me by my Aunt Marilyn White Thompson, youngest sister to my mother, Ledra, when I asked her why the family moved from Iowa to Missouri. She said, as the story was told to her, that her uncle, LeRoy Harsh, asked Albert to move to Missouri because there was a job opportunity working on the railroad. Albert and Vinnie packed up their eight children and moved to Cedar County, Missouri.

Marilyn White Thompson
13th and youngest child of
Albert and Vinnie White

In checking the records, they had ten children, but two little boys died in infancy while living in Iowa. Their tenth child, Marvin, died in February, 1922, in Mount Ayr, Ringgold County, Iowa. In March of 1923, their eleventh child, Thomas White, was born in Fair Play, Cedar County, Missouri.

The family lived in Fair Play, on a cross-roads corner in the country, which to this day is still called "White's Corner." I know because I was there in 2016, and the locals called it "White's Corner." The railroad job fell through, but they farmed the land and made friends. They moved to Macon, Missouri, by 1926. Then, records show they were living in Exeter, California, in 1930.

Fair Play is where mother met my daddy, William "Ethmer" Lynch. They were just teenagers but fell in love and ran off to get married in 1925. Mom once told me how she loved to kiss his big lips. *Luanna*

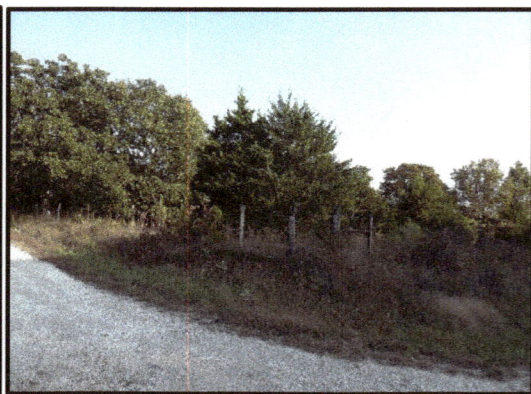

White's Corner where Mom's family lived until about 1926 when they moved to Macon, Missouri. Mom had married Daddy in 1925, and they lived in a little house on his parent's 80 acres in Fair Play. My heartbroken Mom did not see her parents for ten years.

Friends and Family c. 1925, MO

This picture had to be taken not too long before Mom and Dad ran off to get married.

Left to right:
Rushey Lynch, Dad's sister. She married James Thompson.
Ina White, Mom's sister. She married Jess Thompson, brother to James Thompson.
Ledra White, (Mom) Ina's sister, who married Rushey's brother, William "Ethmer" Lynch.
Opal Thompson, best friend to Ledra and was sister to James and Jess Thompson.
Vinnie White, mother to Ina and Ledra.

Wedding Photo
May 19, 1925

Ledra White
And
Ethmer Lynch

Ethmer was 19 and Ledra was 15 years old. The Justice of the Peace wanted to know if Ledra was 18. Ethmer had written the number 18 on a piece of paper and put it in the bottom of Ledra's shoe. Not wanting to lie, he said, "Yes," and didn't feel guilty because she was standing over the number 18 in her shoe.

Newlyweds
Ethmer and Ledra Lynch - c. 1925

I see a black kitten sitting between Ethmer and Ledra. It may have been Mom's idea to have the picture taken with a kitten. I remember so well how superstitious Dad was. He hated black cats because he thought they were bad luck. As a teen, I remember Dad making a dangerous U-turn because a black cat ran across the street in front of our car.

II

Miss Mary

As to why Mother wrote this poem, I have no clue. I know she would write poems for Barbara and Belva when they needed one for a class assignment, but she never told me the reason why she wrote this one. Maybe she was just having fun.

Luanna

Note: Country Folk Talk. You will notice in Mom's poetry and songs, the English language will be different. It's called Country Folk Language. It's a real way of speaking that makes perfect sense to those speaking and hearing it because that was the way they were raised.

When I read the book by Mitch Jane, *Home Grown Stories and Home Fried Lies*, I discovered that the Missourian and the Ozark way of speaking were perfectly normal, as long as you didn't move to California. And then, when enough Missourians moved to California, it was okay as long as they just talked amongst each other.

My sister, Sharyl, and I had a difficult time on many occasions because we were reared in a home of Country Talk. "All stoved up" meant a person's body was stiff. "Sit'n spraddle legg'ed" meant a person was sitting with their legs spread open. "I d'clare" and "All swan," hearing something surprising. This way of talk has nothing to do with the lack of intelligence. If you attended a country school and this is the way the teacher spoke, then what choice did you have?

If a word ended in the letter i, like Missouri, it's pronounced, Missoura. I always thought my aunt was Aunt Vedie, and, in my genealogy research, I discovered she was really Aunt Veda. There is no way you can convince them to speak differently. You are a product of your parents and how they taught you. I'm still a work in progress. I will on occasion get up out of my chair and complain, "I sure am all stoved up today."

Miss Mary
A Poem by
Ledra A. White Lynch
c. 1936

Miss Mary said to write a poem in which I never did.

So I'm going to sketch just these few lines instead.

Mother said poetry is living, just like bees, birds, and flowers.

And of living I am thankful for my loaded, labored hours.

I try to grasp what 'ere I can and abide by the golden rule.

And when I gets to be an old grey haired hag,

me thinks I have reached my goal.

Ledra and Ethmer's first child, Barbara Ellen, was born July 17, 1926 in Dinuba, California.

About this time, 1926, friends started migrating to California. Mom talked Dad into following her friends. It had to be difficult for him since all he had ever known was his country home in Cedar County, Missouri. They didn't stay in California long. Their next two children, Belva and Carol, were born, 1928 and 1929 respectively, in the little two-room house on the 80 acres in Missouri.

Out to California they came again, and Bill was born in 1931 in Lindsay, but James was born in Missouri in 1933. In 1943, Sharyl was born in Missouri, but, by 1945, they had settled in California for good and only made trips back to Missouri to visit Dad's parents, William "Bill" and Effie Davis Lynch. I was born in Visalia, California, in 1947. With six children, it became difficult for Dad to make a living and provide for his family on the farm in Missouri. A permanent move to California was the only solution.

Ethmer with his 1927 Chevy in California

III

The Snow

"The Snow." This may be my favorite of Mom's poetry. Or second favorite next to the "Ojai Valley". Maybe it's a tie. When I wrote this down as Mom recited it, I asked her why she wrote this poem. This is what she related to me.

Belva was about nine or ten years old and attended the Hartley school in the Master's area in Missouri. She had an assignment from her teacher to write a poem, and she just couldn't think of anything to write. Belva said, "Mama, I got to have a poem." Mama said, "I have to fix your breakfast," and went out on the porch to get some fire wood for the stove. Belva began to cry. Mom looked around outside and said, "Hurry, Belva, get a pencil and paper, it snowed last night."

And out came the words to this beautiful poem.

Luanna

The Snow
A Poem by
Ledra A. White Lynch
c. 1937

As I awoke this morning
From the stillness of the night.

God had changed all the surroundings
To a blanket pure and white.

Meadows carved in all their brightness,
Seems like all the world aglow.

Friends I ask thee answer me this question,
What's more beautiful than the snow?

Sharon Moran
11-4-2015

This is the house on the 80 acres in Missouri, where Mom and Dad lived when Mom wrote "The Snow" poem. There was no electricity, no running water, but they farmed and ate off the land. They had large vegetable gardens, cows, horses, pigs, and they churned the cream to make their butter.

Mom told me that Dad reared the boys, and she reared the girls. The boys had rifles, and Dad taught them to hunt.

The old house was obviously abandoned in this photo. Mom gave birth to four of my siblings in this two-room house. I was here in 1965. There was still a part of a fence standing, and there were furnishings inside. I brought home to California an old song book with my Dad's handwriting in it.

I can imagine Mom stepping out on the porch to gather in some firewood for their wood burning stove when she looked around and saw the beauty of a fresh snow on the ground.

**Ethmer and Ledra Lynch
and Their First Four Children**

Left to right:
William "Bill" Albert
Belva Lee
Barbara Ellen
James Ethmer

Baby, Carol Sue, was born between Belva and Bill but passed away shortly after birth. She had trouble breathing. Ten years after James, Sharyl Sue was born; then, four years after Sharyl, Luanna Kay was born.

IV

The Daffodils

Mom could not remember when or why she wrote this poem for Barbara, but she must have been fairly young, I imagine before Barbara was a teenager. But Mom did remember she wrote this for her.

I could be wrong, but I don't remember Barbara or Belva ever writing poetry. Maybe I'm the only one of the six siblings who enjoys writing and composing my own poetry and stories. I never asked Mom to write anything for me. She was my example and I emulated her.

Luanna

The Daffodils
A Poem by
Ledra A. White Lynch
c. 1937
Written for Barbara

There was a little house that stood upon a hill
With white geraniums and yellow daffodils.

They laughed and they played in the bright sunshine.
They even had a party with the morning glory vine.

A little boy and girl they came out to play,
And they picked all the daffodils and throwed them all away.

The morning glory wept and said, "What a disgrace."
They got so disappointed they covered up their face.

Ethmer Lynch's Family c. 1941 Missouri

Ethmer's Parents, William "Bill" and Effie Davis Lynch, are standing in the center back.

Orville Mayse, Gwen Thompson, Billy Lynch, Jimmy Lynch, Ethmer Lynch, Bill and Effie Lynch with Edith Lynch in front, Barbara Lynch, Genivee Mayse Coy, Elmer Coy holding their son, Dale, Liza Lynch Mayse, Rushey Lynch Thompson, and Belva Lynch

Lynch Cousins

Left to right: Genivee Mayse Coy, Gwen Thompson, Orville Mayse,
Barbara Lynch, Belva Lynch
Front: Jimmy Lynch, Dale Coy, Billy Lynch. C. 1941

V

The Upper Ojai Valley

"The orchard trees are white, in the
springtime in the Upper Ojai Valley."

Barbara, Ledra, Belva,
Sharyl c. 1946

Ojai Valley, California

by Luanna Lynch Leisure
Memoir

I have heard many stories about the life and adventures of my family, most of which I never experienced since I am the youngest child. My parents and siblings loved telling stories, especially when we would all be together on weekends and holidays. After dinner we'd gather around, and pretty soon I would hear someone say, "Do you remember when....?" I would sit somewhere on the floor and just listen, taking it all in. Daddy sat in his arm chair, and I would sometimes see tears in his brilliant, blue eyes as they reminisced about the good ol' days.

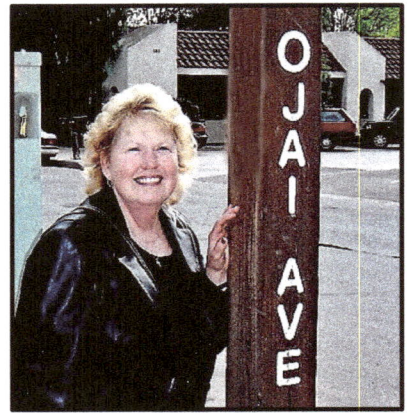

One period of time they particularly liked to relive was their experiences in the Ojai Valley, a beautiful little community with hills and valleys nestled between Ventura, Santa Paula, and Santa Barbara in Southern California. My family lived there between 1945 and 1947. Mom even wrote a song about the Upper Ojai Valley.

For years I was haunted by the memories of the stories and Mom's song of the Ojai Valley. I felt a connection even though I was not born during the time they lived there, so much so, that in 1999 and 2005, my husband, Herb, took me to Ojai as part of two anniversary trips. He was a good sport and helped me trace my family roots.

It was a beautiful drive, and I loved the quaint retirement town of Ojai. There are two main valleys, the upper and lower. The town is nestled in the lower valley, and my family had lived and worked in the upper.

Post card on the left of downtown Ojai is dated April 30, 1947, sent from Mom to Barbara and Rusty shortly after they were married. I took the photo on the right at pretty close to the same spot in downtown Ojai in 2005.

On one of our trips, I called around and found a historian who was a young boy during the 50s. He remembered the people's names and the places I was told by my family. My brother Bill, who was living in Missouri, was especially helpful. The historian joined us in our car, and we went from place to place. I was able to see with my own eyes exactly where my family had lived and worked.

On our 2005 trip, I called brother Bill and he would explain the area and tell me where the sulphur springs were located, and he asked me if it smelled like rotten eggs. He had me experience the 17-mile drive down the Ojai Santa Paula curvy road. Herb put our car in neutral, just like Bill told him, and sure enough we made it all the way down to Santa Paula in neutral.

At one point, Herb got out of our car to take a picture for me and, since I was alone in the car, I sang with gusto Mom's song, "The Ojai Valley." At the end, I cried so hard. I felt close to Mom, and I sang it for her. She wrote it there and sang it there many times.

Herb Leisure Husband and all-around good sport.

The Lynch family, consisting of William "Ethmer," Ledra, Barbara, Belva, Bill, Jim, and Sharyl, moved from Missouri to the Upper Ojai Valley in California in 1945.

During the two years or so they lived there, Mom and Dad worked on the Drown Ranch, which the historian showed me, and I was able to walk around where the apricot trays had been many years before.

Belva, Dixie McBride, Barbara, Rusty, Bill, Sharyl, and friend, Mary in the front.

Jim attended school in Ojai, which was still there. Barbara and Belva decided they didn't want to go back to school and got jobs at the Social Insecteria in Santa Paula. Yes, that was the real name. Belva helped me with these facts.

Barbara and Belva's job description at the Insecteria was to take black bugs, which lived on Irish Potato plants, and put them in little vials. The vials would be taken out to the orange groves, and the bugs would be let loose. The bugs would eat sap-sucking insects called mealy bugs, which attacked oranges.

As related to me from Bill, he would drive Barbara and Belva to work and then drive himself to school in Santa Paula. He was not old enough to drive, and he couldn't see over the steering wheel of the 1937 Pontiac, so he would sit on a pillow and coast down the winding, narrow road. With the car in neutral, he'd skid and squeal that Pontiac all the way down the 17 miles to Santa Paula. In spite of his reckless driving, he got his first ticket for not having a driver's license.

Barbara & Belva
Ojai 1946

Even though the school announced that no one was to skip school to go fishing, Bill and his friends played hooky anyway on the opening day of trout season. Some things were just more important than school. Bill got sixty days detention for his indiscretion, and he wasn't able to pick up Barbara and Belva from work. After a couple of days of detention he decided to quit school.

When the apricots ripened, crews were brought in from all around to pick the apricots. After they were picked by the work crews, my family pitted them and placed them on drying trays. Mama even made the girls quit their jobs to work with the apricots. Bill's job was to drive a 1934 pickup and dump the pits into a ravine by the hillside. Life wasn't all work though. Many times they would all go down to Ventura and spend the day at the beach.

Life also changed for the family while living in Ojai. Belva married Robert Findley, Barbara married Rusty Gannaway, and after doing the math, **lo and behold, I discovered I was conceived in the Upper Ojai Valley.**

Left: The Drown Ranch. Ethmer, Ledra, Unknown lady, Barbara, Belva, and Dixie McBride.
Right: Fun on the Ventura Beach. Rusty, Barbara, Dixie Dean McBride, Belva, and Ledra.
Looks like they were all trying to fit on the same blanket. c.1945-1947

Note: In stanza three, of Mom's song, she writes, "Just step on your starter. . . " For those who may not know, the older vehicles did not have a key to start the engine, you stepped on a starter on the floor.

The Upper Ojai Valley
A Song by
Ledra A. White Lynch
c. 1946
Pictures taken in the
Upper Ojai Valley

There's a land that I love and it's nestled high above
Where there's no broad streets or no alleys.
Where the sun shines so bright and the orchard trees are white
In the springtime in the Upper Ojai Valley.

Oh, the Ojai Valley,
The Ojai Valley,
Where the deer they hop and spring
On the rattlesnakes that sing
In the springtime in the Upper Ojai Valley.

Oh, if you love the mountains and I am sure that you do,
And if you love a place that will drive away the blues,
Just step on your starter and say, "Come on old Sally,"
For we're gonna take a trip in the Upper Ojai Valley.

Oh, the Ojai Valley,
The Ojai Valley,
Where the deer they hop and spring
On the rattlesnakes that sing
In the springtime in the Upper Ojai Valley.

Oh, when my maker He comes and calls for me,
I'll say to my Master, "I've been waiting for thee."
Just add up my column and see if it don't tally,
Then bury my bones in the Upper Ojai Valley.

Oh, the Ojai Valley,
The Ojai Valley,
Where the deer they hop and spring
On the rattlesnakes that sing
In the springtime in the Upper Ojai Valley.

The Upper Ojai Valley

Ledra Lynch

andante moderato

There's a land that I love and it's nest-led high a-bove where there's
no broad streets or no al-leys where the sun shines so bright and the
orch-ard trees are white in the spring-time in the Up-per O-jai
Val-ley Oh! the O-jai Val-ley the O-jai Val-ley where the
deer they hop and spring on the rat-tle-snakes that sing in the
spring-time in the Up-per O-jai Val-ley

Ledra White Lynch
On the Drown Ranch
c. 1945

Picture on the left: See Barbara on the tractor and Belva standing on the other side.

My husband, Herb, wrote the score to Mom's song and music. I sang the song like Mom did. He played it on the piano and wrote the score.

VI

Annie and Sam

The following is what my mother told me, Luanna, in 1993.

Sam and Annie Agnew Thompson lived in Lindsay, California. On April 25, 1946, Sam shot and killed his wife, Annie.

Sam was Jim, Youlas, Opal, Jess, Ida "Idie," and Nellie Thompson's brother. Jim was married to Daddy's sister, Rushey, and Jess was married to Mom's sister, Ina.

Sam shot Annie because he was jealous. He thought she was running around with George Depew. George was married to Idie, Sam's sister. George chased after Annie, but Annie would have nothing to do with George. This caused lots of arguments and fights which ended with the death of Annie. Mother was so grieved over Annie's death she wrote this ballad. At this time in 1993, Mom was still grieving over such a senseless tragedy.

Note: Following is a little more to the story by family member, Rolayne Edwards.

"Sam and his wife were separated. Sam went to his bartender and asked to borrow the bartender's gun. When the bartender asked him why, Sam said he needed it to kill his wife. Apparently, that was enough of an explanation for the bartender because he gave Sam his gun. Sam used that gun to shoot his estranged wife.

Sam was sentenced to five years to life in San Quentin prison for second-degree murder. This was probably the result of a plea bargain since the facts above if accurate left little doubt this was first-degree murder. Another of Sam's sisters (Jewel) was married to a man with considerable political clout in those days and I have always wondered if that was a factor in the light sentence and early release as well.

When Sam was released seven years into his sentence, we were living in South San Francisco. Whatever possessed Hershel, my step-father, to pack up his wife, six, four and two-year-old children and take the two-hour trip to pick up this murderer/uncle in the dead (excuse the expression) of night still puzzles me.

I remember the night was so dark. That was probably because we must have travelled Highway 101 which would have taken us through miles of farmland back in the 1950s. We had a dark green Chevrolet sedan with a bench front seat. Sam sat in the middle between my stepfather and mother when we left San Quentin. I do not remember much conversation on the way home."

Note: Following is a little more to the story by family member, Carolyn Thompson Nouar.

My grandmother, Alean Thompson, was close with Annie and was devastated when she was killed. She said Sam believed Annie and George Depew were having an affair. I will tell you that my grandmother was a Christian woman and she didn't like talk of things like that, the affair, etc., and when she was telling me she did say that she didn't like to believe that Annie was doing that but maybe she was. She loved Annie and when Sam killed her, she was distraught and she did her best to keep their daughters in her life and wrote them and they wrote her cards and letters through the years.

My grandmother said that Sam was waiting for Annie to come out of her house as she was going to work and he shot her when she got to her car. She had a large sum of money $1300 - $1400 in her purse and it was still in her purse when they found her so they knew it wasn't robbery. After Sam shot her, he drove to my grandparents' house and said he had shot her and told Grandpa that the sheriff would be looking for him and that he was going to drive south towards Bakersfield on highway 65.

Note: Following is a little more to the story by family member, Terry Gardner.

I will never forget the day when we went to visit Aunt Ledra for the last time. We were all sitting around in a circle at her care home, I remember Ledra's daughter, Barbara, was there and my parents. Anyway, Aunt Ledra was not talking, only listening, and then all of a sudden she burst forth singing the song she wrote about Sam and Annie. Ledra too was close friends with Annie. Up until that day I had no idea that Aunt Ledra wrote such wonderful poems and songs or that she had a beautiful singing voice. Wonderful memory!

Annie Thompson Shot To Death On Way To Job

Ex-Mate In Hospital Under Police Guard After Head-On Crash

Mrs. Annie M. Thompson, about 50, was murdered early this morning as she was leaving her orange ranch home near Lindsay, and a short time later her estranged husband, Sam Thompson, was removed unconscious from his automobile following a head-on crash near Porterville and held for the crime.

Mrs. Thompson, her body riddled with three bullets, was found lying half on the ground and half in her car in the driveway of her home on Ash avenue two and one-half miles northwest of Lindsay this morning. The shooting, called murder by Sheriff S. B. Sherman, took place shortly after 7:30 a. m., apparently as the dead woman was preparing to leave for Lindsay, where she worked as an orange packer.

Sam and Annie (McAbee) Thompson abt 1910

Thompson Enters Surprise Plea Of Guilty To 2nd Degree Murder Of Estranged Wife

Sam H. Thompson, 60, yesterday afternoon at 3:55 o'clock entered a surprise plea of guilty to second degree murder in the death of his wife, Annie, at Lindsay last April, and was sentenced to San Quentin state prison by Judge Glenn L. Moran, in superior court. Penalty on the charge is from five years to life.

District Attorney Walter Haight explained that the state was willing to accept the second degree murder plea, instead of the first degree with which Thompson was charged, because it was felt that there would be no difficulty establishing the fact that Thompson was grossly intoxicated at the time of the crime, precluding his ability to form intent. Premeditation is essential to first degree murder.

Thompson withdrew his previous pleas of not guilty and not guilty by reason of insanity, and faltered slightly as he pleaded guilty on the second degree charge. Immediately after, however, as he answered routine questions put by the district attorney concerning his background, he spoke firmly and loud enough for all the few spectators to hear every word.

He gave his name as Samuel Henry Thompson, said that he was born in Missouri and attended school only a few days.

At the age of 21 he left his father's farm, where he had worked without pay, he said, and for thirty years followed the power and telephone line construction trade, serving many years as construction boss. Asked about any injuries received during his lifetime, he admitted to a broken jaw and said many years of lineman's work had broken his arches, which caused him, a big man, to walk with some difficulty.

Trial on the charge that he murdered his estranged wife, Annie M. Thompson, last April 25 had been set last Monday for July 24 by Judge Moran. At his arraignment June 24, Thompson had entered pleas of not guilty and not guilty by reason of insanity through his attorneys. Arraignment was continued for setting of trial at that time.

Thompson was accused of the murder of his wife as she left her small orange ranch home on Ash avenue two and one-half miles northwest of Lindsay about 7:30 the morning of April 25. Shortly after the shooting she was found half in and half out of her car riddled with three slugs from a high-powered .38-caliber revolver.

Later in the morning Thompson was taken into custody by highway patrol officers investigating his crash into a concrete bridge at Deer Creek two miles south of Porterville. They found the revolver, later identified as the murder weapon, in his car. Thompson was

(Continued on Page Three)

Compromise For Terminal Pay Proposed

Truman Suggests Using Government Bonds As Part Of Huge Amount

WASHINGTON, July 9. (AP)—The senate military committee today endorsed a White House-approved plan to use government bonds, as well as cash, in paying approximately 14,000,000 war veterans for accumulated furlough time.

Committee approval clears the way for probable early senate action which members forecast will be favorable.

WASHINGTON, July 9. (AP)—The White House said today President Truman has proposed a compromise plan to use government bonds, as well as cash, in paying approximately 14,000,000 war veterans for accumulated furlough time.

The plan, Press Secretary Eben Ayers told a news conference, is the president's own idea. Under it, veterans who served in the ranks would get cash for all terminal leave payments less than $50 and five-year bonds in $25 denom.

Thompson Pleads
(Continued from Page One)

unconscious and drunk when removed from the accident scene.

He denied all knowledge of the crime when questioned in county jail, but admitted drinking heavily early the morning of the fatal shooting. He persisted in denying knowledge of the crime later, also.

Robbery was early eliminated as a motive for the shooting as $1375 was found in Mrs. Thompson's purse by investigating officers. Neighbors reported hearing quarreling immediately preceding the shooting.

A charge of first degree murder was filed by the district attorney's office, and Thompson was held to answer to superior court on the charge by E. B. Gould in Lindsay justice of the peace court on May 31.

He has been held in county jail since his arrest, except for a brief period when first apprehended, when he was under guard in county hospital.

BULLET, GUN LINKED IN LINDSAY CASE

Ballistics experts in Sacramento have established that the spent .38 caliber bullet found under the body of Mrs. Annie Thompson was fired from the gun which was later found in the car of her divorced husband, Sam Thompson, at Lindsay, April 25, it has been announced.

Time for the preliminary hearing in the Lindsay justice of the peace court is expected to be set this week, but is dependent upon the arrival of the ballistics expert, who will testify. If sufficient evidence is produced at the hearing Thompson will be automatically bound over for superior court trial, District Attorney Walter Haight said following a coroner's inquest.

Annie and Sam

A Ballad by
Ledra A. White Lynch
c. 1946

Way out in California
in that far distant land,
there lived a middle aged couple,
whose names were Annie and Sam.

Many years they lived together
and toiled as man and wife,
'till quarrels grew quite frequent
and Sam took Annie's life.

They had two beautiful young daughters.
Oh, God, have pity I pray,
for they loved their mother and father,
no difference could they make.

They wept by their mother's casket,
there was nothing they could do,
while father was in his prison cell
awaiting for his doom.

If Sam could have stopped his drinking
and Annie been more fair,
these grief stricken daughters and kin folks
would not have had this to bear.

Continued next page

But the devil and all his wickedness,
he had his own cruel way.
If God had of been in this household,
there'd not have been this today.

In day's gone by was a prayer from all the Christians,
"Oh, Father guide the young,
but did you ever think of the mothers and fathers
and the cruel things they've done."

And you who are in habit of drinking
getting drunk and going astray,
you ought to know in this great wide world
you'll never get by that way.

You'll find out sooner or later,
you've made one great mistake,
and that when the going gets too rough
it's usually then too late.

Just one more prayer for the mothers and fathers,
"Oh, God, oh help them live right,
and be with the friends and loved ones
of Annie and Sam tonight."

Sharyl Sue Lynch Justice
Daughter of Ethmer and Ledra Lynch
Long View, Texas

**Bill and Sharyl Lynch Justice
Daughter, Kim Justice Johnson, and
son, Darin Justice**

I have wonderful memories when all our family would come to visit Mom and Dad in their little house on Stevenson Street. I remember well how my brothers would sit on the back side of the kitchen table against a window, in a very small, cramped space with Dad on one end and others sitting on the other sides. The rest of us would sit around in the living room where we could find a place. They would talk about the old times with Dad and Mom and they would all laugh and have a good time. Luanna and I would sit on the floor and listen to their stories. We enjoyed hearing their stories over and over. We never got tired of them.

I remember Mom was so clean. She would mop, scrub, and clean the walls. When the house needed it, she would even paint.

When I was small, I remember in Missouri, Mom washed clothes in a big tub over a fire. She would boil the clothes and scrubbed them clean on a wash board, then she hung the clothes on a barbed wire fence to dry. Mom also made homemade lye soap out of lye and ash. In California she was able to have a ringer washer. I can remember doing the laundry on that ringer washer and I also remember putting a piece of red clothing in the tub and all the clothes turned red, but Mom didn't get mad at me.

When I would go on a date, she would say, "You be good." The problem was, we never had the conversation about what she meant. I just knew I better be good. Then she would tell me, "You just remember, you are just as good as anybody else, but you are no better than anybody else." She would also say, "Quit your belly ache'n." She would say this if I was complaining about something or if Luanna and I were fussing at each other.

Mom was a hard worker. When surprise company would drop by, she would jump up and immediately bake a pie. She always had fruit that she had canned.

Luanna Kay Lynch Guy Leisure
Daughter of Ethmer and Ledra Lynch
Campbell, California

Mom was a survivor. She endured many hurts and hardships over the years, but there were many wonderful times too. She always loved her children and grandchildren. They were a delight to her, and she loved to feed them. But, the most difficult time in her life was when Daddy died.

On that sad day, the family was over and, as usual, Mom had fixed a wonderful meal. Daddy was not feeling well. They had just returned several days previously from a trip to Missouri where Dad had an emergency hernia surgery and was still recovering. I was engaged and was planning a wedding for the next

Herb and Luanna Lynch Guy Leisure Daughter, Tracy Guy Herlofson; Granddaughter, Tessa Herlofson; Grandson, Tanner Herlofson; Son, Tommy Guy; Granddaughter, Haley Guy, and son, Jimmy Guy, dad of Haley.

month. I left the house to go visit my soon-to-be-in-laws. When I arrived, I had a call to rush back home. When I drove up, I saw Daddy being put in the back of an ambulance. He died of a massive heart attack that night on August 6, 1967.

Mom was paralyzed with grief. She was in shock. As you read through the pages of *Ledra's Book*, you will see the years of devotion and love the two had for each other. They were children when they married, and, through all the good and difficult times, they never once stopped loving each other.

Gradually she began to start living again. She had faith in God, which helped her, and she had all of us kids too. When my husband was drafted to Viet Nam, Mom made me move back home. It never entered my mind to not do what she said, even though I loved my little apartment.

As time went by, can you believe it, she even had a date or two. I would call her to make sure she made it home okay. The tables were turned, but it was so good to see Mom enjoying life. Her strength gave me strength when I went through a divorce many years later. She was there for me and my children, a safe haven, comfort, and always a good meal of fried chicken and peach cobbler. "Thank you, Mama."

VII

Mother's Prayer

Growing up, I always remembered a picture of Jesus on a wall in our home. Jesus was holding a small, frail lamb with sheep following all around Him. Mom loved that picture and would many times gaze at the picture on the wall. She never prayed out loud that I can remember, but, in her mind, and heart, I know she would cry out to God. When I think more about it, sometimes when she would pray I believe it came out in song, like this song she wrote in about 1948.

I'm curious to know what was going on in Mom's life and why she felt so sad when she wrote this song. My sister, Sharyl, remembers me being a baby, just a few months old.

Mom always believed in God and looked to Him for her help. And, children don't always know what their parents are going through.

After she wrote this song, Mother dedicated it to RB Walters and Pearl Gannaway Walters, the stepfather and mother to Harold "Rusty" Gannaway. Rusty was my sister Barbara's husband. RB was a Pentecostal minister and Mom wanted it sung at church. As I remember, her wish was granted.

Luanna

Mother's Prayer

A Song by
Ledra Anita White Lynch
c. 1948

I dedicate this to RB and Pearl
Walters to sing as a special at church.

I was sad and forlorn and I thought my Lord had gone,
Would not hear me when I cried.
As I knelt there in prayer so deep in despair
I thought to my soul I'd surely die.

Then I heard a faint voice say,
"Weary one look this way,"
And I gazed at a picture on the wall.
And I hung my head in shame as I heard him call my name
For I had not looked upon it in many a day.

There my Jesus stood with a halo or'e his head
And a weak weary lamb in his arms.
And the fold followed close beside
With the great Shepard as their guide
Knowing that to them there would come no harm.

Oh, the Lord is my Shepard I shall not want.
He maketh me to be satisfied.
If to him you will atone
Put your faith in him alone
Call upon Him and you will not be denied.

So if you stray from the fold
And get lost in the pages of sin
If upon him you will call
And rely on His sweet voice
Like that weak weary lamb He will bring you in.

Sisters, Aunts and Niece
c. 1948

To understand this title, I must explain. Sharyl, in the middle, and I are sisters. I am on the left (Luanna). On the right is Beverly, she is our niece, the daughter of Belva, our next to the oldest sister.

Sharyl said she remembers that when I was a baby Mom had the picture of Jesus on the wall, and thinks she may have written her song sometime around then. We were living in Exeter, California, at the time. Mom had that picture for years because I remember seeing it in our home until she could no longer live on her own.

Mother and Daughter
Ledra and Luanna

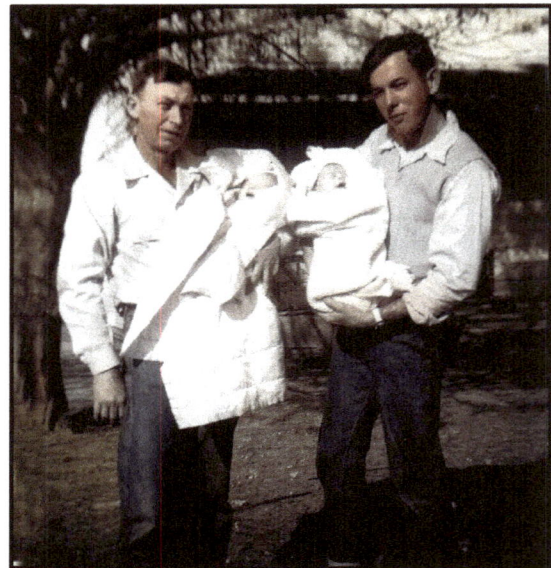

Daddy Daughter and Daddy Daughter
Left: Ethmer and Luanna: Daddy - Daughter
Right: Robert and Beverly: Daddy - Daughter
Ethmer and Robert: Father-in-law - Son-in-Law
Beverly to Ethmer: Granddaughter - Grandpa
Luanna to Robert: Sister-in-Law - Brother-in-Law
Luanna and Beverly: Aunt - Niece

Mother Daughter
Ledra and Luanna

VIII

Gosh, I Wish I Was a Belgian

This, to me, was a very odd jingle. When I expressed my feelings to Mama the following was her explanation.

In 1918 the Germans oppressed the Belgians, and the United States gave clothes to the Belgian people. Many of the U.S. citizens were poor and did without. Someone wrote this jingle in protest against the Belgians getting new clothes instead of the U.S. citizens.

A fact from Wikipedia:

The history of Belgium in World War I traces Belgium's role between the German invasion in 1914, through the continued military resistance and occupation of the territory by German forces to the armistice in 1918, as well as the role it played in the international war effort through its African colony and small force on the Eastern Front. **Nov 4 2019**

I did an extensive search for copyright laws and "Gosh, I Wish I Was a Belgian" was not listed in the alphabetical listing of WWI songs and poetry. It may have been written by someone local in Iowa where my mother and her family lived during WWI.

Mom said when she was about nine years old and the news came that the war had ended (1918), she ran outside and clapped her hands and jumped up and down yelling, "We beat, we beat." Her Aunt Minnie Harsh Mull was there and said, "Ledra, say we won."

Aunt Minnie was a sister to Vinnie Harsh White, Ledra's mother.

Luanna

Harsh Siblings
c. 1958

Ledra's mother's maiden name was Harsh. Vinnie Harsh White. Here is Vinnie with her siblings.

On the end, far right, is Minnie Harsh Mull, Ledra's Aunt. She was the one who instructed Ledra to say, "We won."

Left to right: Leota Harsh Hogue, Claude Harsh, Vinnie Harsh White, Ralph Harsh, Leola Harsh Miller (twin to Leota), and Minnie Harsh Mull.

Gosh, I Wish I Was a Belgian

Recited by
Ledra A. White Lynch
Author Unknown, c. 1918

Gosh, I wish I was a Belgian.
I'd have lots of clothes to wear.

Gosh I wish I was a Belgian.
People sewing for me everywhere.

We'd have new clothes and a brand new shirt.
I'd be a regular gosh darn flirt.

Gosh, I wish I was a Belgian.

Ethmer and Ledra White Lynch with Their Six Children
c.1955, Madera, California
Back Row: James, Barbara, Belva, and Bill
Front Row: Sharyl, Ledra, Ethmer, and Luanna
I was missing my front teeth and didn't want to smile.

Sisters
The two youngest children of
Ledra and Ethmer Lynch

Luanna Lynch and Sharyl Lynch
c. 1951
Rocky Hill Ranch,
Exeter, California

Mom always told Sharyl to take
care of me. Thank you, Sister, for
always being there for me, and
sorry I always gave you so much
trouble. I was a rascal and very
independent.

IX

Long Boy

When I asked Mother for the title of this little ditty, she said she didn't know. All she knew was it came out during WWI.

After some research, I discovered it was a popular song during that time. I found the cover page and sheet music online. Even though it was a song, Mom would recite not sing it.

Thankfully it is public domain material as stated on the website and on my copyright page.

Luanna

Long Boy
Recited by
Ledra A. White Lynch
Lyricist William Herschell, c. 1917

He was just a lean long country gink,
Way out west where hop toads wink.
He was six foot two in his stocking feet,
And he kept a getting thinner the more he'd eat.

"Good bye Maw and goodbye Paw,
And goodbye mule with an old hee haw.
I may not know what this war is about,
But I bet, by gosh, I'll soon find out.

And, oh, my sweet heart don't you fear,
I'll bring you a king for a souvenir.
I'll get you a Turk and the Kaiser too,
That's about all one feller can do.

Good bye Maw and goodbye Paw,
And goodbye mule with an old hee haw.
I may not know what this war is about,
But I bet, by gosh, I'll soon find out."

One pair of socks was his only load,
When he struck for town down the old dirt road.
He went right up to the public square,
And fell in line with the soldiers there.

Sergeant put him in a uniform,
His gal knit mitts for to keep him warm
They drilled him long,
And he sang his farewell song.

"Good bye Maw and goodbye Paw,
And goodbye mule with an old hee haw.
I may not know what this war is about,
But I bet, by gosh, I'll soon find out."

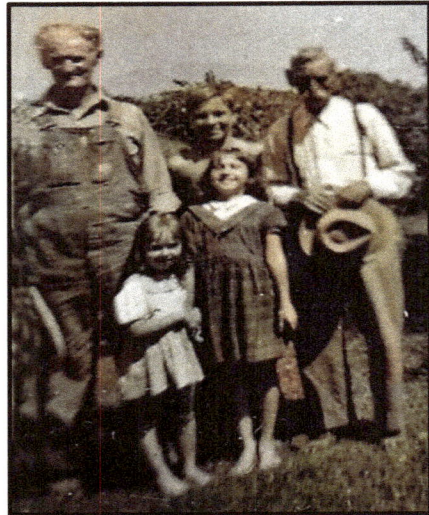

Grandfathers
Left to right: Grandpa, Albert White; first cousin, Richard White; Grandpa, William "Bill" Lynch; and sisters, Sharyl and Luanna

Sisters
Top photo left to right: Luanna and Sharyl Lynch
Rocky Hill Ranch, Exeter, California, c. 1952
Bottom photo left to right: Sharyl Lynch Justice and Luanna Lynch Leisure
Gladwater, Texas, c. 2019

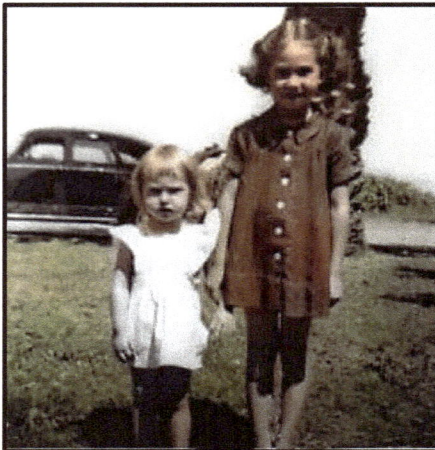

Luanna and Sharyl, Rocky Hill Ranch, Exeter, California, c. 1950

X

Railroad Crossing

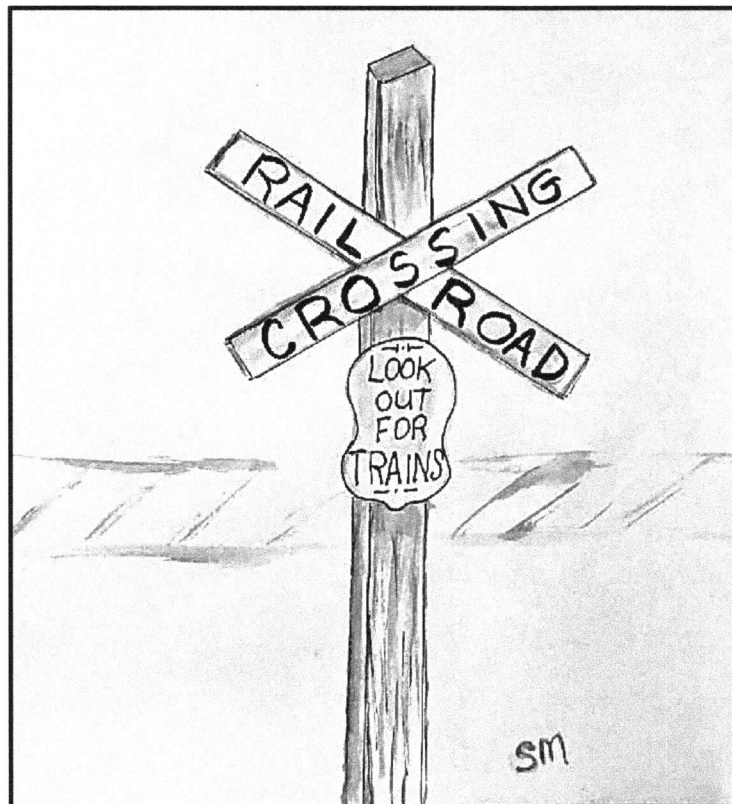

Another jingle Mom loved to recite. My internet search was futile when it came to finding the author and publication date. Searching by typing in a line or two usually takes me right to an author, but not for this one.

Mom learned this as a child. I wish I knew who taught it to her, but sadly there is no one left alive to ask.

Luanna

Sharing Memories of Grandmother

Ledra and Ethmer had six children who grew up to be adults. From these six children, they were blessed with 14 grandchildren. Then, these 14 gave Ledra and Ethmer 25 great grandchildren who added to the family tree 33 great-great grandchildren. As of today, Ledra and Ethmer have eight great-great-great grandchildren. Total of, let's do the math, 86 descendants. Not bad for a young couple who married at ages 15 and 19. I'm sure on the day they eloped, it never entered their minds that their union would lead to that many children, and children's children, who are all a blessing for Ledra and Ethmer. A beautiful, loving family.

My son, Tommy, Ledra's youngest grandchild, mentioned to me some of his memories of his grandma. "What a good idea," I told Tommy. In the following pages, scattered throughout here and there in *Ledra's Book*, are memories and photos from Ledra and Ethmer's grandchildren. Thank you, Debbie, Connie, Janice, Bobby, Kathrine, Bill, Mike, Darin, Kim, Tracy, Jimmy, and Tommy for sharing your memories of your Grandma, and thank you Tommy for your great idea. This makes your grandma's book complete. If Beverly and Karen were still with us, I know they too would have had some wonderful memories of their own to share.

Railroad Crossing

Recited by
Ledra White Lynch
Author Unknown

Well, you see I started down to town with that 'ere team of mine,
And I was haulin' down a load of grapes to Ebenezer Cline.

Well, you see the railroad cuts across down there at Martin's hole,
And there I saw a great big sign stuck high upon a pole.

Well, I felt kind of curious, I liked to find out what it said,
And so I stopped the horses on the railroad track and I read.

Well, I'm not no scholar, recollect, and so I had to spell.
And so it started kind of curious like with R A I L R O A D.

Railroad, that 'ere much I knowed. C R O S S and I N G to boot.
Well, that spelled railroad crossing just as plain as Noah dared to do it.

Well, L O O K was look and I was a looking, too,
And I was just spellin' like a book. O U T, out,

When something came along and just gave me an awful whack,
And it knocked me right off that railroad track.

The horses went to Davy Jones. The wagon went to smash,
And I was tossed a 50 yards above the tallest Ash.

I never come to life again for about a day or two,
Though I was crippled up a heap I sorta struggled through.

Now it ain't the loss nor it ain't the gain of that 'ere team of mine,
But how I'd love to know the rest of that 'ere sign.

Memories of My Grandmother

Deborah Annette Gannaway Townsend
Daughter of Rusty and **Barbara Lynch Gannaway**
Kilgore, Texas

One main memory I have was when Grandpa Lynch passed away. I lived in Woodlake with Mom and Dad but I went to stay with Grandma for a week. She was very sad and depressed and lost without Grandpa. I said, "Grandma, let's play ball." So she agreed and we got down on the floor and we just rolled a ball back and forth to each other. It seemed to help her. I also remember the old feather bed we cousins would sleep on when we would go over for a visit. I remember helping Grandma stuff it back into the little hall closest shelf at the very top. We would shove and squish it into the cubby hole. Once, I remembered when I helped Grandma pick peaches off her tree in her backyard. I stepped on a rotten peach barefoot and the peach was full of bees and I got stung several times. Interesting the things a person remembers.

Debbie's Family
Top left: Mike and Debbie with sons, Chris, Joshua (1985-2002), Robert and Troy.
Top Right: Abby, Mike, Chris holding Kaceson & Braxton, Nena, Debbie, Brooke.
Bottom Left: Camille, Troy, and baby Merida.
Right: Mike, Debbie, Robert, Janet, Tarver, and Cheyenne.

XI

Old Charlie

Poor Old Charlie. Kind of a sad poem, but Mom enjoyed reciting this with much inflection and intonation.

This is another poem I could not find the author or date of publication. Mom knew this since childhood. She grew to despise alcoholism. *Luanna*

Memories of My Grandmother

Beverly Ann Findley Warren
In Loving Memory of Beverly
1947 – 2019
Daughter of Robert and **Belva Lynch Findley**
Lemoore, California

Beverly's Family

Left to right: **Beverly** far left. Steve Warren and Beverly's daughter and son, Becky Cagle Murrietta and Troy Cagle. Troy's wife Laurie and their three children, Bret, Shay, and Katie. The two children on the left are Bev's grandchildren, Annalee and Raymond Murrietta. Picture to the right is Beverly's son, Billie Gene Cagle, his wife Christina and children, Zack, Julie, Harlegh, Ali, and Zac.

Note: Beverly and I were born at the same hospital just a few hours apart. My mom and sister were giving birth to us at the same time. Yes, this was unusual. We were more like twin sisters, and her death devastated me. *Luanna*

Old Charlie
Recited by
Ledra A. White Lynch
Author Unknown

It was only last Sunday in a mile of my course,
Nobody being present but me and my horse.

It was the first time I knew that old Charlie could speak,
When I cracked him over the head with a stick.

"Why?" he says, "Why do you abuse me, for you are a man?
I'll pack your journey as fast as I can.

Over hill and over hollers and other rough ground,
I'll pack your journey and never give down.

When you are sober you feed well, I know.
You feed lots of roughness and ride might slow.

But when you are drunk you holler you squall,
You ride like the devil and feed none at all."

Connie Sue Findley Ayers
Daughter of Robert and **Belva Lynch Findley**
Stockton, Missouri

I loved breakfast at Grandma's. She would fix the best oatmeal, biscuits and gravy. Oh, my, gosh, it was wonderful. And grandma's pies were the best. I also remember how beautiful her dogwood tree was out in her front yard. She brought it back from one of her trips to Missouri when it was just a twig all wrapped in wet paper towels and placed in a plastic bag. It was happy where she planted it because it grew into a beautiful tree that had pretty blossoms. I also remember Grandma's featherbed and the time Beverly and Luanna fluffed it all up ready for us to sleep on. It was not easy to do and it took them a long time. When they walked out of the room, Janice and I rolled and played on it until we had flattened it all out. As I remember we got in trouble.

Ledra standing in front of her Dogwood tree. Visalia, California c. 1987

Connie's Family
Left side: Randy and Connie Fndley Ayres with Connie's mom, Belva Lynch Findley. Right side: Connie and Randy's daughter and husband, Ray and Shawna Ayres Vier, and twin grandsons, Robert and Randy.

XII

Little Man From Durham

A limerick poem. From whence it came? Maybe Mom would have known, but I doubt it. I can imagine Mom at school, having fun with her friends learning and reciting silly poems and singing silly songs. She loved to do this.

Alas, I searched diligently and could not find author or publication date. I don't think this was literature for a class assignment. Definitely tongue in check. Just an outrageous little lyric the kids of the day had fun reciting.

Such fun songs during my grammar school days were similar. "Do Your Ears Hang Low;" "I know a Wiener Man;" "Jimmy Crack Corn;" "Kookaburra;" "Oh, Susanna;" "I Went to the Animal Fair;" "Little Blue Man;" "Alice, Where are You Going?;" "My Gal's a Corker;" "I'm a Nut;" "You're a Grand Old Flag," and many, many more. I called my niece, Connie, for her help in remembering the songs we sang. She talked with her sister, Janice, and, between the three of us, we remembered quite a few. It was fun reminiscing.

My nieces, Beverly, Connie, and Janice Findley and I used to sing and perform as kids. We had a blast. Beverly and I were the same age, Connie and Janice younger. Our parents and family would be inside visiting, and we would be outside singing our hearts out. I do remember on one occasion, late in the evening when we were particularly loud, they yelled at us to be quiet because the whole neighborhood could hear us. It dampened my spirits somewhat because I thought we were really good at entertaining the neighborhood instead of annoying them.   *Luanna*

Siblings, Aunts, Uncle, and Nieces
Exeter, California c. 1953

Standing in back is Bill Lynch, my brother.

Right to left: Sharyl Lynch Justice, my sister.

Beverly, Luanna (me), Connie and Janice, nieces.

We were a little bit older when we did our performing.

Little Man From Durham
Recited by
Ledra A. White Lynch
Author Unknown

There was a little man from Durham.
He bought a pair of pants and he wore 'em.

He stooped and felt quite a draft,
And knew right where he tore 'em.

Uh Oh!

Memories of My Grandmother

Janice Lee Findley Stevens
Daughter of Robert and **Belva Lynch Findley**
Coarsgold, California

I remember Grandma had a photo album that was on a small stand. There was a knob I would turn to flip through to look at the pictures. Grandma would sit next to me and I would ask her, "Who are the people in the pictures?" She would tell me and I enjoyed this time with Grandma. Also, I remember she had a peach tree in her backyard and when the peaches were ripe I helped Grandma pick the peaches.

Janice's Family
Top left: Terry and Janice Findley Stevens with grandson, Kyle. Terry passed away in August of 2018. Right top: Janice and Terry's children, David, Christy Chinn, and Jennifer Stevens. Bottom: Michelle Zender, Michelle Stevens, wife of David Stevens, and sons, Jacob, Kyle, and David. Mike Morris and his daughter, Madison. Janice in front with daughter, Jennifer, and her son, Joshua.

Robert "Bobby" William Findley
Son of Robert and **Belva Lynch Findley**
Clinton, Missouri

I have so many memories of Grandma. On Sunday after church we would go to Grandma's to eat, visit and play with cousins. It was where the family went. Grandma would have fried chicken and peach cobbler. Everything was so good. Sometimes after church I remember going out to Mooney Grove Park. On occasion we would stop at A&W with Grandma and I loved the hamburger and root beer float.

On Thanksgiving the house would be full and the adults would sit around the table in the kitchen and us younger kids would sit at a card table in the living room. I remember playing out in the yard with cousins Darin, Billy and Mike.

Robert and Jean Findley

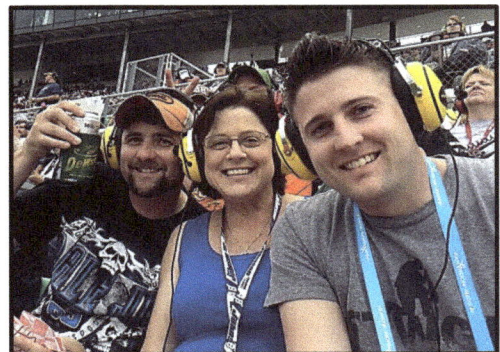

Grandma had an old antique sewing machine and an old iron that was so heavy she would use it to prop open the door. It was made out of cast iron. What was so funny and I remember it so well, Grandma used to say, "All swan." She would say this when she would get excited over something someone said.

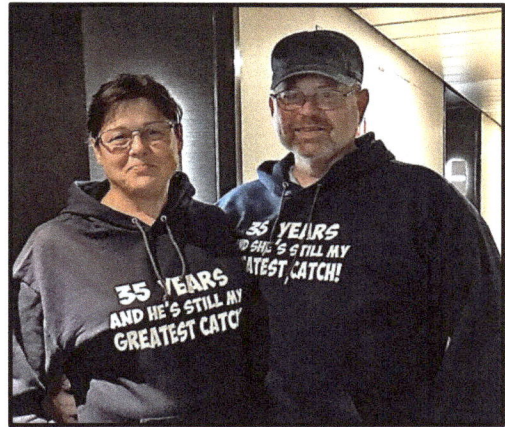

Robert's Family
Far left: Robert, wife Jean and son, Eric. Middle: Ian Findley, son of Eric and Whitney Findley.

Right: Eric, Jean and Brian. Wife and sons of Robert Findley.

Genealogy Tree

Cousin Sharon, painted this grand old tree. It makes me think of our family with the deep roots from generations gone by and the sturdy trunk from the mix of our parents and grandparents who hold us up strong and glue us together. The strong limbs are the next generation and the smaller are the next as we look to our future generations and keep on growing. Families are the ties that bind.

Luanna

Memories of My Grandmother

Katherine "Kathy" Jean Lynch Grover
Daughter of **William "Bill" Lynch** and Dorothy Batemen Lynch
Nixa, Missouri

I believed my Grandma Lynch worked magic in her kitchen on Sundays in 1965 when I was a 10 year old child. On Sundays, my mother would take my two brothers and me to church and afterwards to Grandma and Grandpa's house for lunch. While we were at church, my father loved to go to Grandma's (his parents) to drink coffee, talk of life, politics and moving to Missouri. I was always excited to see my extended family of aunts, uncles and cousins who would all show up throughout the afternoon.

My Grandma would cook all Sunday morning and through my child's eyes her efforts looked so easy. She would fry several chickens, make biscuits and gravy, mashed potatoes and all the trimmings. I will never forget her pies and cobblers that completed the feast. Every Sunday was like a holiday.

As a child I took this family gathering for granted. As an adult, I have no idea how she had the energy to work hard all week at her job, clean house and shop on Saturday, then cook for her entire family all day Sunday. She must have had great endurance and energy. If I could talk to my Grandma Lynch one more time at my current age

Kathy's Family
Front: Kathy holding granddaughter, Willa Romesburg; her mother, Dorothy Bateman Lynch; grandson, Liam Romesburg. Back: Gary Grover, Paul and Gunda Romesburg, Stephen, and Brittney Grover (daughter) Romesburg; son, Bryan (not in picture).

of 65, I would tell her how much of an impression her hard work, sacrifice and loving acts of kindness created in me. I would tell her how thankful I am for her bringing us together on Sundays and creating my beautiful childhood memories of family and belonging. She created the magic of family in her small kitchen and for this, I will always be grateful.

When I was 11 years old my parents moved our family to Missouri, far away from our family in California. It was difficult to purchase nice fruit during the winter and as a Christmas gift to our family, Grandma would ship a huge box of oranges. The box would be placed under the tree and we would eat them throughout the season. The oranges were juicy and delicious and the odor would waft throughout the house.

William "Bill" Albert Lynch Jr.
Son of William "Bill" Lynch Sr. and Dorothy Batemen Lynch
St. James, Missouri

Bill's Family
Bill and Marg Lynch
Caralee, and Anna Lynch

The first thing I immediately remember is Grandma's delicious peach cobbler, then all the family gathering at Grandma and Grandpa's. I can still see the big smile on Grandma's face when we all gathered in the house. It made her so happy to see us.

The holidays were great. I remember exchanging Christmas presents and the lights on the Christmas tree. The 4th of July was special because of the fireworks and lighting the black snakes on the sidewalk and driveway with our cousins. Happy memories.

Michael "Mike" John Lynch
Son of William "Bill" Lynch and Dorothy Batemen Lynch
Manchester, Missouri

I remember if Grandma had 20 guests in her house she would cook for 40. Always lots of food. The cream corn, green beans, ham and chicken, everything cooked in that small kitchen and the house smelled wonderful, like baked bread. She would have cake, cobbler, watermelon and cantaloupe and sometimes we would eat outside.

Grandma loved her family and she was the glue that kept the family together. I remember once she drove to Woodlake to see Barbara. Billy could drive but Grandma had to do the driving. It was foggy out and she counted the streets to find their house. A little scary. Grandma was a testament of the human soul and endurance. No matter what she went through her heart guided her life. She had grit and determination all of her life.

Michael's Family
Mike and Veronique Lynch
Nichola, and Arrielle Lynch

Karen Diane Lynch Ramsey Goldstone
In Loving Memory of Karen
1960 -2011
Daughter of **James Lynch** and Geraldene Dixon Lynch
Oxford, Connecticut

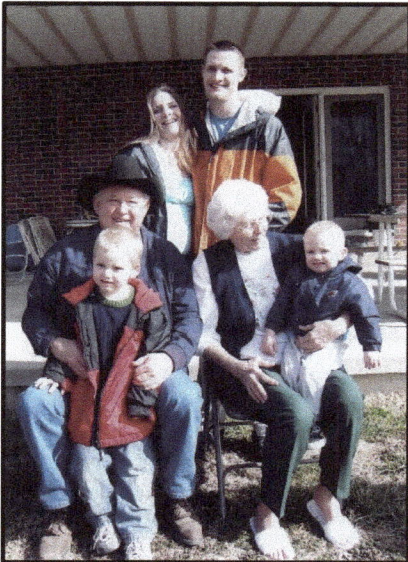

Karen's Family

Right: Karen with her son, LJ Ramsey.

Left: Karen's parents, James and Geraldene Lynch; Grandsons, Orion and Aydin; son and wife, LJ and Angie Ramsey.

Darin James Justice
Son of Bill and **Sharyl Lynch Justice**
Princeton, Texas

As a kid, probably around the age of twelve, I remember Grandma paying me to mow her lawn. Can't remember how much, but it seemed like a lot at the time. Then she got me a job mowing a lady's lawn who seemed about Grandma's age, who lived across the street. I thought I practically had a business going. I remember a few occasions in the beginning, mowing with a no-engine push mower that Grandma had.

Another great memory was going to Grandma's house on any special occasion for family. Cousin, Bobby and I, and whoever else happened to be there, played football in the front yard and across the neighbor, Flo's yard.

Darin and wife Ruth

Continued on page 68

Darin James Justice, Continued

Darin's Family

Left to right: Terry and Kim Justice Johnson; Darin's parents, Bill and Sharyl Lynch Justice; Darin and his wife, Ruth Hart Justice.

Eating chicken and gravy and drinking iced tea. . . I would tell Grandma, "I can't eat anymore," and she would put another chicken leg on my plate. She would always tell us we weren't eating enough, even though we were stuffed to the gills. On these family get-togethers, we also heard many great stories about Missouri. As a kid I thought Missouri had to be the best place on earth. It snowed there and you could hear the whippoorwill birds.

I loved Grandma's gravy. One time she was talking in the kitchen to those helping her, and someone who was helping her had a runny nose and it dripped into the gravy. She told those that were working with her in the kitchen that this person said they got it out (the nose drip) with a big spoon before it did any harm. Being the nosey over-hearer that I was, this turned my stomach against gravy for several years after this.

Last memory. . .

I remember Mom, Kim and me walking down Main Street in Visalia with Grandma. I was a teenager at the time. We were waiting to go across the crosswalk. When the signal flashed "WALK," My mom grabbed Kim's hand – no big deal. Grandma then grabbed my hand and I freaked out. Looking back now, I wouldn't have freaked out and made the scene I did then. I understand why the younger me didn't want Grandma to hold my hand, but at the same time, it's still such a great memory and fun for me to still think about.

Thanks for the laugh in the older me now, Grandma!

Memories of My Grandmother

Kimberly "Kim" Ann Justice Gilbert Johnson
Daughter of Bill and **Sharyl Lynch Justice**
Gladewater, Texas

I have so many great memories of Grandma Lynch. Anyone who had ever been to Grandma's for a meal knows you never go home feeling hungry. Even though you would be full, she would always try to get you to eat a little more. Grandma made the best chicken and dumplings, and the best fried chicken. Grandma was the number one chef when it came to comfort food. I also remember Grandma having a relationship with God. She always had a Bible around, regularly went to church, and would sing the song, Amazing Grace. Grandma Lynch was fun, smart and entertaining. I sure miss Grandma.

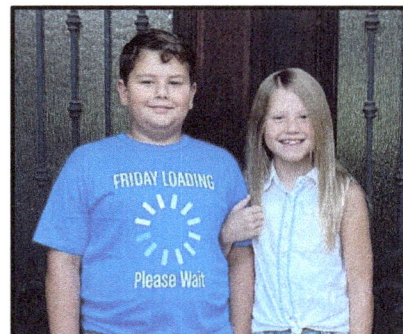

Kim's Family
Right top is Megan Gilbert Hendrix; Terry and Kim Justice Gilbert Johnson; Micah Gilbert; Nathan Johnson. Bottom left: Jeremy Hendrix holding daughter, baby Caroline and Megan Gilbert Hendrix; Terry and Kim Johnson; Lauren Johnson Farnham, and her daughters, Rosalyn and Jacquelyn. Right bottom is Kiyler and Keylie.

Memories of My Grandmother

Tracy Kay Guy Herlofson
Daughter of Greg Guy and **Luanna Lynch Guy Leisure**
Mesa, Arizona

If you were going to go see Grandma, don't eat because as soon as you arrived she would ask, "Are you hungry?" No matter your answer, you would soon be eating. I would sit at her kitchen table and watch her cut up a whole chicken and fry it in oil. Somewhere between me running out the back door to explore and being called back in, the fried chicken was done along with mashed potatoes, gravy, homemade biscuits, something green and of course, homemade peach cobbler.

The peaches came off her tree in the backyard. If it wasn't peach cobbler, then it was her scrumptious persimmon cookies.

In the summer her kitchen was as hot as it was outside on a summer California day. So where would Grandma be after eating? Standing under the swamp cooler putting on a clean blouse and trying to cool off. These are the wonderful, heartwarming memories of my Grandma Lynch that I will never forget. Love you always, Grandma.

Tracy's Family
Left: Tracy and children, Tessa and Tanner Herlofson. Photo taken in Italy, 2019. Right: Tracy and Todd Herlofson, Todd passed away in 2013, and their children, Tessa and Tanner.

James "Jimmy" Ethmer Guy
Son of Greg Guy and **Luanna Lynch Guy Leisure**
Visalia, California

Chicken and dumplings was my favorite meal at Grandma's. Tommy and I would stay with Grandma when Mom took college classes at night and I loved it because she would always fix us something good to eat. The only problem I had was in the winter she would heat up the house to what felt like 1,000 degrees. Her house was so small and I couldn't breathe it was so hot. All she had was a small floor heater, but it sure could heat the house.

Jimmy's Family
Left: Jimmy and Cristina Rodriguez

Right: Jimmy and his daughter, Haley Guy

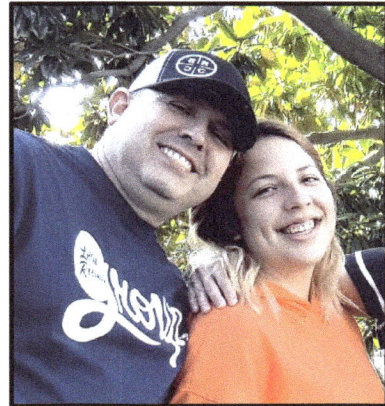

Thomas "Tommy" Gregory Guy
Son of Greg Guy and **Luanna Lynch Guy Leisure**
Campbell, California

What I remember most is Grandma's delicious chicken and dumplings. I couldn't stop eating them. My stomach would hurt because I would eat so much. Grandma used to say funny sayings, like, "All swan" and "I d'clare." Sometimes Grandma would be on the phone and exclaim, "All swan." I never knew what it meant, but I will always remember Grandma's old-time sayings.

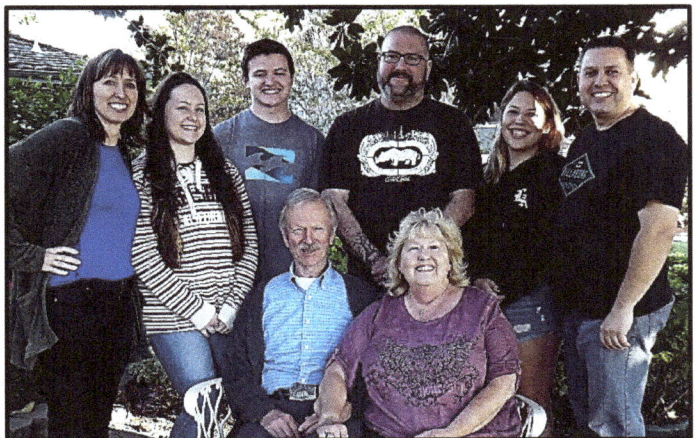

Tommy's Family
Tracy, Tessa, Tanner, **Tommy**, Haley, Jimmy
Mom and Dad (Luanna and Herb)

Ledra White Lynch
and her six children, c. 1990
Back Row: Bill, Belva, Barbara, and James
Front Row: Luanna, Ledra, and Sharyl

Ledra and Ethmer's Six Children

The previous pages hold some dear memories from Ledra's grandchildren, the children of her children in the above picture.

Mentioned earlier, Ledra and Ethmer had six children who grew to be adults. Those children gave them 14 grandchildren, and they blessed Ledra and Ethmer with 25 great grandchildren. Then along came 33 great-great grandchildren and as of right now, Ethmer and Ledra have eight great-great-great grandchildren.

About the Poet and Song Writer

Ledra Anita White Lynch was born in Iowa in 1909 and was the fourth child of Albert and Vinnie Harsh White. From the stories she told about her childhood, she loved school and was eager to continue her education. Unfortunately, the high school was too far away from their home in rural Iowa. This was very disappointing for her. She was also needed at home to help with her younger siblings.

Her parents had 13 children, of which 11 lived to be adults. She loved her brothers and sisters and once said if anyone picked on her brothers at school she would beat them up.

Ledra was good in math, history, reading, recitals, and good old common sense. She worked hard next to her husband who had health problems, doing all she could to protect and help him. She married William "Ethmer" when she was only 15 ½, and Ethmer had turned 19 four days prior to their wedding. When they stood before the Justice of the Peace, he asked if Ledra was over 18 years old. Ethmer had planned ahead, because he didn't want to lie. He had put a piece of paper in Ledra's shoe with the number 18 written on it so he could honestly say she was "OVER" 18. They ran away to get married which grieved her parents. Even though they were young and you would think the marriage would fail, they celebrated 42 years together when Ethmer passed away in 1967.

Ledra and Ethmer had seven children of which six lived to be adults. She served as Noble Grand in the Rebecca Lodge and was an active member of the Visalia Senior Center. She was never shy to perform and entertained in plays, dances, and, even on occasions when the group took the show on the road to perform for other cities and organizations. She would perform and dance the Charleston. All her life she was gracious, and hospitality was her strong suit. She would feed family and friends on a regular basis.

She was a strong and determined lady who always fought for what she believed was right, and she lived by the golden rule.

Ledra and Ethmer
40th Wedding Anniversary

May 19, 1965
Visalia, California

They married when Ledra was 15
and Ethmer was 19 years old.

Ethmer died August 6, 1967
Ledra died January 19, 2000

Ledra with her son,
James Ethmer Lynch
c. 1980

Mom enjoyed dressing up and
attending the Rebecca Lodge. She
participated in many events for
several years with her daughter,
Barbara, and her sister, Marilyn.

Ledra's Parents and Siblings
Albert and Vinnie Harsh White,
and their Eleven Children

Albert and Vinnie Harsh White
and their Eleven Children c. 1947
Back Row: Hallie, Thomas, Luther, Dorleigh, Elvis, Harry "Bob," Earl.
Front Row: Marilyn, Ledra, Albert and Vinnie, Ina, Clarice.

First Cousins c. 2005

Four in this picture are not in the picture below. Combining the two photos here are 13 of the 33 first cousins.

Left to right: Kenneth White, Steven White, Sharon Thompson Moran, Deborah White Santana, Gary White, Luanna Lynch Leisure, Dennis White, John White, Diana White Brown, Tom White and Mark White.

First Cousins c. 2014

Nine of 33 Grandchildren of Albert and Vinnie White

Top photo taken at Uncle Dorleigh White's Memorial. Bottom photo taken at the 70th Wedding Anniversary of Avery and Marilyn White Thompson.

Left to Right: Pamela Thompson Loop, Diana White Brown, Thomas White, Sharon Thompson Moran, Gary White, Luanna Lynch Leisure, Dennis White, Julie White Ross, and Steven White.

About the Author
Luanna Lynch Leisure

It had been my dream for many years to publish a book for Mother. As I started compiling her poetry, ideas kept coming and now it is more than just her poetry. Included are family photos, genealogy, Cousin Sharon's art, as well as my thoughts (memoirs) on Mom's writing. To add the icing on the cake, the grandchildren have written memories of their Grandma.

I am the youngest child of Ethmer and Ledra Lynch. Being the youngest, I did a lot of observing, and I learned much from my siblings and parents. Sharyl and I grew up together, and life was different from when our older siblings grew up. We stayed settled in California, and only a few trips were made back to Missouri as a family. Thankfully, my husband, Herb, has taken me on several trips to visit family and to trace my family roots. How many enjoy using their vacation time to visit old cemeteries to take pictures of headstones? I do! How many already have their headstone up in the Hartley family cemetery in Missouri. I do!

My fondest memories are being with cousins and nieces. I loved the family get-togethers and Mama's fried chicken and peach cobblers.

I'm a genealogist, publisher, writer, and author. I've published three children's books, *Mystery at Lone Oak Ranch; Quack! Quack! I Want My Feather's Back;* and *Best Buds.* I've also published a book of memoirs for the members of a memoirs class I attend. I've been a part of Louise Webb's Memoirs Class since 2012. *Ledra's Book* is my fifth published book. Only thing good coming from the Covid-19 Pandemic is having the time to write. My books can be purchased at LuLu.com and Amazon.com

National League of American Pen Women is an organization of professional women in the Arts. I've been a member in the Santa Clara County Branch since 2012, and I am the current president. I'm also a photographer, and my membership is in Writing and Art. Come visit me at my **website: www.LuannaLeisureBooks.com**

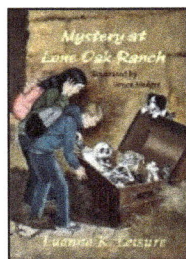

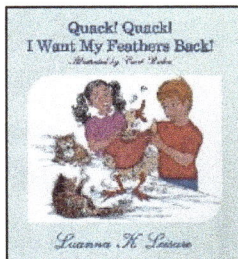

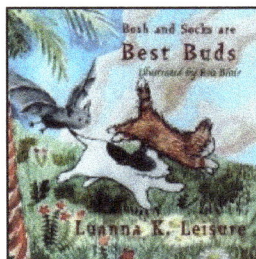

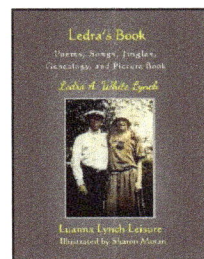

About the Illustrator
Sharon Thompson Moran
Family Photo March 14, 2014
70th Wedding Anniversary of Avery and Marilyn White Thompson
Sisters, Sharon and Pam with parents, Avery and Marilyn Thompson

Thank you again, Sharon, for taking so much of your time to create and paint the illustrations for your Aunt Ledra's book. You went above and beyond.

Sharon's whole family is artistic. Her sister, Pam, also enjoys taking art classes and is an excellent artist. The girls come by it genetically because their mother, Marilyn, was also a wonderful artist and had her paintings hanging on the walls in their home. Sharon's dad, Uncle Avery, worked with wood and could make everything from park benches to wooden napkin holders. A very talented family. Love you dear family and I miss my Aunt Marilyn.

Luanna

About the Illustrator
Sharon Thompson Moran

I am the oldest daughter of the youngest child of Albert and Vinnie White. Ledra Lynch was my Aunt, my mother's older sister, and Luanna Leisure and I are 1st cousins. Growing up in a family with 11 siblings and 33 cousins was a wonderful way to grow up. Family gatherings were always big and boisterous and fun.

I began watercolor painting after I retired, and really loved the creativity. When Luanna asked if I would do some illustrations for Aunt Ledra's poems, I was thrilled. Her poems are so lovely and will be a treasure to have in book form. Although I am not a great painter, I had fun with these illustrations, and I hope you enjoy our endeavors.